COMMON SENSE
FOR
BOARD
MEMBERS

40 Essays about Board Service

Edgar Stoesz

Good Books

Intercourse, PA 17534
800/762-7171 • www.goodbks.com

Design by Dawn J. Ranck

COMMON SENSE
Copyright © 2000 by Good Books, Intercourse, PA 17534
International Standard Book Number: 1-56148-319-2
Library of Congress Catalog Card Number: 00-050288

Library of Congress Cataloging-in-Data Publication

Stoesz, Edgar.
        Common sense for board members : 40 essays about board service / Edgar Stoesz.
            p. cm.
        ISBN 1-56148-319-2
        1. Boards of directors. I. Title.
        HD2745.S78 2000
        658.4'22-dc21   00-050288

Table of Contents

Foreword

" . . . never thought a man lost time by stopping to sharpen his ax."

—Abraham Lincoln

Board service is not a science with formulas that consistently produce a predictable result. Board service is mostly a matter of common sense. But what is more uncommon than common sense? The scene that repeats itself in boardrooms daily is well described in the German proverb:

Everybody does what they will,
No one does as they should,
But everybody is fully engaged.

Board service is like jazz—you experiment until you find a chord that works, and then you play it for all you can. Board service is frequently an exercise in creative pragmatism.

These essays are short and to the point because most directors have limited reading time. Keeping each essay to two pages allowed me to cover many subjects which confront boards, although it precluded my doing so in detail.

Wanting this book to benefit from the insights of other practitioners, I invited critical comments form the following: Ruth Daugherty (United Methodist committee women); William E. Dunn (CEO and chairman); Karen Foreman (Habitat executive and lecturer, Organizational Development professor at the University of Washington); Chester A. Raber (consultant, author); Dean A. Stoesz (my son, a for-profit manager). Their helpful comments have been incorporated and are hereby gratefully acknowledged, along with the editorial contribution of Phyllis Pellman Good who helped to make the text more understandable.

My purpose in writing this book is to make service on a board more effective and enjoyable. I have found that there is ample room for both.

— Edgar Stoesz
Fall, 2000

The Role and Duties of a Board

Getting Board Service in Focus

The Board's Role

Why do most nonprofit and church boards spend more time in meetings than boards of large corporations like General Motors? It is because most nonprofit boards do not distinguish between governance and operations. They burn themselves out doing administrative work while neglecting their primary function, which is to govern. This distinction is illustrated in the diagram below.

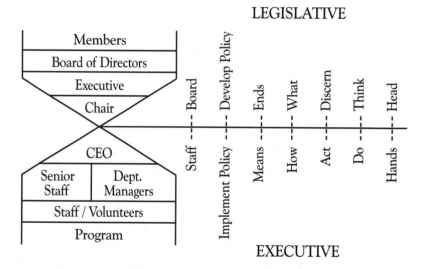

A board's first duty is to govern, to determine the ends for which the organization exists. It is to discern, to think, to exercise judgment, to plan. Implementation of board actions is delegated to staff or committees, based on board-approved policies. Board work is head work. Hands are optional.

This is not to suggest that governance is more important than operations, or that an impenetrable wall separates the two.

Think of it more as a partnership based on mutual respect. Directors may and should monitor what is going on below the line. Staff is invited to help the board with its governing function. The German proverb describes the ideal: "One hand washes the other." There are two hands, each with its own function.

Board members may be involved in operations. They may sell popcorn at the annual fund-raiser, but they do so under the authority of the person in charge (board or staff). Their "help" must not be at the expense of their primary board function, which is to govern. Directors, to quote Mohammed Ali, do not have license to "float like a butterfly and sting like a bee."

Young or small organizations usually do not make this distinction. Everybody works until the work is done, or they fall over from exhaustion. As organizations grow and mature, boards need to have less hands-on involvement and to concentrate on governing. Failure to do so results in overburdening the board, while leaving staff uncertain about what is expected of them. Instead of leading, boards excessively involved in operations are perpetually on the verge of burnout.

When this distinction is understood and practiced, board work is more effective. Meetings are shorter, more productive, and enjoyable. It all begins with the board grasping a clear understanding of its role and directing its focus accordingly.

The next six essays describe the primary duties of a board. These are functions a board must do, and competent boards do all six to at least 90% optimum effectiveness.

Purpose

Why does this organization exist?

Organizations exist to do, to accomplish something. A board's first duty is to define what that is. Boards do this by asking the following questions:

1) What do the members who elected us expect us to do? Why are they supporting us?

Member expectations are seldom in written form, but they exist. Bylaws usually have a section on purpose, but their intent is to satisfy a legal requirement. Organizations need a purpose statement which is dynamic and keeps them focused on why they exist.

Directors can surmise what their members want by what they support, by whom they elect, and by what they say informally.

2) What is needed? What are our opportunities? What is our niche? Needs abound, and so do nonprofits to address them! There are in the United States some two million nonprofits, all specializing in something. Habitat for Humanity specializes in building decent, affordable houses with and for deserving families. Others do cultural or historic work, like the Society for the Preservation of Covered Bridges. On a local level are active schools, clinics, and camping programs.

Directors must identify the need to which they feel called, consistent with member expectations.

3) What are our resources? What do we know? What can we do? What do we have or what can we get by way of staff, money, or material? Many nonprofits are tempted to want to be all things to all people. They chase popular causes. They overestimate themselves and underestimate what is needed. Nothing is served by do-gooders undertaking something which is outside their competence or resources.

Against this background, effective directors focus on two things: vision and mission.

VISION is what an organization wishes to *become*. In defining its vision an organization lifts itself above everyday limitations and frustrations and asks itself, what do we want to become? They dream of something in the future.

The best vision statements are bold and concise. They help keep an organization focused and motivated.

The American Leprosy Mission enthusiastically adopted the following vision statement: "Christ's servants, freeing the world from leprosy." Those seven short words say much about who the Leprosy Mission is and what it wants to accomplish.

MISSION is what an organization commits itself to *do*. Whereas vision is a dream, a stretch, mission is a commitment. "This we will do." Habitat for Humanity says, "Building houses with God's people in need." Mission is grounded in the here and now; vision reaches for the stars. Organizations need both.

Until an organization has a clear and compelling sense of purpose, it wanders. It remains tentative and lacking in focus. When an organization clarifies its purpose and commits to it, its limits will be determined only by the energy it can give to achieving that purpose.

Planning

How will the organization's purpose be achieved?

After a board has clarified its purpose for existing, it must devise a plan to achieve it. Vision and mission statements are only fine-sounding phrases until they are put into operation.

Surviving another year is all many directors are concerned about. Having done that, they congratulate each other and courageously face another year. That is not good enough. Organizations exist to *do*, and for that they need to *plan*.

Planning is the link between what is and what is to be. Organizations need both a long-range plan and an annual work plan. The two are related but distinct. The long-range is a dream. It is visionary. It is general. It consists of ideas. It reaches beyond what is possible today and states what the organization intends to become.

Vision drives out the status quo. It liberates organizations from the old routine and gives them a reason to exist. It makes room for the future. In the words of Robert Browning, "Our reach must exceed our grasp or what's a heaven for?"

The annual plan is a commitment: "This we will do." It spells out the specific activities by which the mission will be realized. The annual plan states what, who, where, how much, by when, with what (budget). It can be monitored and measured.

These two kinds of planning work in concert with each other. The long-range plan gives directors permission to explore what is beyond their immediate capabilities. It creates a longer term context for annual planning. The annual work plan is, by way of contrast, specific. It is the contract by which directors make good on their promise to perform stated services for the members.

Planning stimulates activities. It permits leaders to anticipate what will be needed to realize a fixed goal. It identifies the facilities and financial and staffing capabilities needed to fulfill identified commitments. It helps to anticipate where a shortfall may occur and permits adjustments accordingly. Plans should be bold but within the realm of what is possible.

Many boards do not have planning in their annual routine. Their agendas are organized around what I will call *organizational housekeeping,* instead of what they want to accomplish. Moving from housekeeping to *planning* in board procedure is not easy. It requires time and discipline, but the reward is increased effectiveness.

Average boards orient themselves around the rearview mirror; precedent is their guide. Good boards examine everything under the microscope; they want to avoid mistakes. Great boards look through a telescope to the planets beyond—at what could be.

Essential as a plan is, the process of planning is even more important. Plans are static, but planning is dynamic. President Eisenhower was fond of saying, "The plan is nothing; planning is everything." Tom Peters warns in a similar vein against holding plans too tightly. Plans can and should be changed when circumstances suggest.

Delegating

Who is responsible?

After they have clarified the organization's purpose, after they have devised plans by which the mission and vision will be realized, board members' next step is to delegate the all-important function of implementing.

Boards may themselves do all the implementing. That is their right, if they have the energy. Some very good organizations have no staff; directors do everything themselves, often making extensive use of board committees (e.g. PTAs, young/small organizations). This is permissible as long as the board does not neglect its governance function.

The role and authority of committees should be spelled out in writing, and it should be understood that committees are subordinate to the board

I enjoyed telling the Habitat board when chairing the meetings, "My job is not to build houses. It is to build an organization that will build many houses." Boards must resist the temptation to reserve more functions to themselves than they can perform without neglecting their governance function.

A board's second option is to delegate implementation of its actions to staff. Boards, it should be recognized, employ directly only one person—the Chief Executive Officer (CEO). All other staff are employed by and report to the CEO. How the board treats its CEO, therefore, sets the tone for the whole organization. A board owes its CEO three things:

1) A job description—what is the CEO responsible for?
2) An annual evaluation—how well is the CEO performing?
3) Support—recognizing that there will likely be disagreements!

Directions to implement require accompanying instructions, also known as policies. Policies are instructions for the future, based on experience and judgment. John Carver, widely respected author on board governance says, "No board activity should take place without reference to policy." Before a board begins the process of approving a budget (or an annual plan), it ought to adopt a policy which states what should be in the budget, who should participate in its preparation, and what its approval procedure will be. Policies permit an organization to learn from experience and to be more efficient and consistent: "We tried that and it doesn't work!"

The Mennonite Central Committee's disaster response policy stated simply, Our response is first through people, then through money. A few words helped staff know that money was not to be sent until staff had assessed the situation on the scene.

Board policies set the parameters within which staff is free to function. If policies are too restrictive, they frustrate and end up being ignored. If they are too general, they leave too much to discretion. When a problem arises with a given policy, the policy should be amended as necessary, but all major activity should be regulated by board-approved policy.

Organizations should organize their policies in a Board Policy Manual for quick reference. Policies are helpful only if they are readily available. When an activity or situation begins to occur regularly, a policy statement should be produced, setting forth how to respond to it.

Having assigned responsibility for the implementation of their plans, with accompanying instructions (policies) as necessary, directors should step back and let it happen. They should not interfere or micromanage. They should not meddle or second-guess. They should observe, always asking, "Is our mission happening? How could it happen better?"

Resources

With what?

Boards are legally and morally responsible to protect their assets, both ledger (meaning money and facilities) and non-ledger (meaning staffing and reputation/image), and to use them to fulfill their identified mission. Boards hold in trust. Not everything is under their control, but everything that does or does not happen is their responsibility.

Ledger Assets

In addition to protecting the organization's assets, boards are responsible to insure that adequate resources are available to carry out the plan they approved. Related functions (fund-raising, accounting, etc.) may be delegated to staff or committees of the board, but *responsibility* resides with the board. To approve a plan or budget without the requisite resources in hand, or without a realistic plan to raise them, is irresponsible. Board members are also expected to support the fund-raising effort and to contribute personally in proportion to their means.

Boards are responsible to ensure that sound financial management is being practiced. This includes:

• Commissioning an independent financial audit annually, including processing the resulting report diligently. (Accountability)

• Approving an annual budget and monitoring experience. (How money is distributed)

• Practicing good risk management. (Exercising a reasonable standard of care)

• Monitoring cash flow. (Insuring that resources are available to meet obligations)

Non-Ledger Assets

This responsibility is divided into two areas:

Personnel: Organizations, we know, are only as good as the people in them. When an organization has good people, most of the rest follows. Good organizations have the ability to attract and retain good staff. The board is responsible to put five mechanisms in place on behalf of personnel:

• Job descriptions for all positions. (Who is responsible to do what?)

• An organizational chart. (Who is responsible to whom?)

• An annual performance appraisal procedure. (How well are staff members doing? How could they do better?)

• A salary and benefit scale, including a plan of growth for all employees. (How much pay/benefits?)

• A grievance procedure. (What to do when things go wrong, as they occasionally will.)

Image-Reputation: "A good name is better than precious ointment," says the Good Book. Indeed, for publicly supported charities, reputation is more valued than the most prestigious credit card. A good reputation is earned over many years and can be lost in one careless act. It is no longer enough to do a good job quietly. It is increasingly necessary for charities to promote their public image. People believe what they are predisposed to believe, and they direct their giving accordingly. Image needs to be built, protected, promoted. It is one of the most valuable assets a public charity has.

Survival is not assured. To serve, an organization must survive; to survive, an organization must serve. Survival does not mean just getting by. To be healthy, organizations must thrive. Obsolescence and apathy must be avoided like the plague.

An organization is rightfully judged by how successful it is in generating resources and in how effectively it appropriates them to achieve its identified mission.

Monitoring and Evaluating

Is it happening?

It is not enough for boards to approve and delegate. Directors must continually ask themselves, is it happening? Is the organization having the desired result? Are we delivering on our "contract" with our members? In answering these questions, directors should not be too superficial or self-congratulatory.

Monitoring—Are the board's instructions being carried out? Directors have numerous sources of information:

• *Their own observations.* Board members should get as close to the action as possible without, however, getting in the way. They should look for appropriate opportunities to visit the office or project sites. Habitat for Humanity International rotates its board meetings to include an overseas locations every second or third year to make it possible for directors of an international organization to have an international experience.

• *Staff reports.* Boards should insist on getting information needed to discharge their board responsibilities, in understandable form. Such reports must offer meaningful comparisons. Most boards don't need more information; they need right information!

Directors should read staff reports appreciatively, but also with a measure of skepticism, knowing the tendency to underreport failure and over-report success. They should be wary when all is suddenly quiet. Perceptive directors read not only what is on the line, but also what is between the lines.

• *Outside audits.* External audits are routine in the financial area. Why aren't they used more in other areas? Such audits may take either of two forms. Periodically a professional consultant may be invited to do a review. Some boards and staff resist this idea because of the cost involved, but if even one useful idea comes out of a consultation, it is worth it. Others resist because they mistakenly think it is a sign of weakness. To the contrary, these reviews can be a sign of strength. "Here is an organization serious about improvement."

Evaluating—Are the organization's activities having the desired effect? Are they hitting the mark? Sometimes the results from an action far exceed the investment made; sometimes the results fall far short. Is a heavy investment in advertising, for example, leading to substantially increased sales? Boards need to evaluate three things:

1) Themselves (begin with the evaluation boards are least willing to do!):
• How is the board functioning? Is it on its toes or dozing? Trees die from the top!
• Is the board making decisions or just approving reports? Are its decisions good ones?
• Are meetings productive or a trial to endure?
• Is the board engaging the future or living on past laurels?
• Is the board providing for its own continuity and/or transition?

2) The performance of the administration, particularly the CEO. A review should include the following:
• Affirmation
• Areas for growth/improvement
• A review of salary, benefits, training, tenure
Administrative reviews should be summarized in writing and reported to the board in executive session.

3) The program. Remember, organizations exist to do.
• Is the mission happening?
• How could it happen better?
• What is winding down or wearing out? (vulnerabilities)
• What is waiting for its turn? (vision, opportunities)
• Are we well positioned for the future?
The process is completed when the evaluation results have been incorporated into the annual planning process.

Reporting Back
to the Membership

What was accomplished?

"**P**urpose—Why does this organization exist?" The second essay, on pages 8 and 9 of this book, states clearly that directors do not own the enterprise. The members do, and that includes donors. It follows logically, therefore, that directors are responsible to report back to the "owners." In so doing they should report not only what was done (activities), but also what was accomplished (outcomes). To put members at ease, the report should include an abbreviated version of the audited financial statement.

Organizations with a local membership are able to do this in person. Such an occasion also affords the board another opportunity to thank the members for their support. The program for the members' meeting should include content, but also human-interest features. Formal business, while important, should be kept to a minimum. Some organizations get good results by serving a simple meal.

Organizations whose membership is geographically scattered must resort to written reports. Here nonprofits can learn from the for-profit world. Stock companies address their annual reports to the stockholders. The nonprofit equivalent is to address the annual report to the membership.

Addressing members as "owners" carries with it a strong psychological message. It reminds directors of their accountability as trustees. This accountability is appreciated by the members and deepens their sense of connection to the organization.

Reporting to the membership includes some strong practical

benefits. Fund-raisers know that current contributors are their best prospects. Most contributors give to numerous charities. How much they give to each depends on how they feel personally about them. Effective reporting builds confidence and trust and earns an organization the right to ask for continued, even increased, support.

Reporting must be honest. It must include failures as well as successes. This becomes a challenge in a down year. Trusting the membership with a disappointment can, in fact, have the effect of deepening trust and support. To the contrary, when problems are glossed over or ignored, the membership becomes cynical and suspicious.

To insure that the duty of reporting to members is adequately accomplished, it should be included in the calendar of board activities and reflected upon in the annual board evaluation.

Money and effort invested in a well informed membership should be viewed as a "cost of doing business" expense. It is not an optional fringe activity; it is an organizational duty.

The last six chapters (Essays 2 through 7 on pages 8-19), summarize a board's role. We turn now to the adjustments directors may face in increasing their effectiveness. This may involve changing habits, some of long-standing, and that is never easy.

The most important decision is the decision to start. Start where you are, with what you know. Make a list of things to be done; then do them. Once in the "habit," the challenge of deliberately carrying out board responsibilities becomes one of doing it year after year, bigger and better. "How much freight can we move over this railroad?" Everything is in place. Needs are there aplenty. People of goodwill are ready to go to work. It starts with the board knowing and discharging its role.

"Directors hold others accountable,
but they, too, are accountable.
Their accountability
is both legal and moral."

— from *Serving "On Your Behalf"*

How
Boards Function

Boards

A Cultural Melting Pot

We come to board service as we are. We think and act out of our varied backgrounds. When you think about the diversity on most boards, it is a wonder the members can agree on anything.

Some directors are accustomed to an enterprise which is under their immediate, daily supervision. They interact with their employees daily. When an issue arises, they meet with the principals directly involved. A decision is made and implemented immediately. An international nonprofit has a very different decision-making process and communication chain.

Many nonprofit directors work in the for-profit world. They are used to a unionized work force instead of volunteers. They are programmed to think of the bottom line and market share. Unless these differences are consciously acknowledged and understood, directors who think in for-profit terms are in danger of addressing nonprofit issues from a perspective that is not helpful.

Directors grow up in, and model themselves after, different leadership styles. One may be shaped by a very authoritarian atmosphere, while another may have grown up in a permissive atmosphere. One has a very controlling supervisor while another is hands-off. All this has a profound psychological effect on how each of us as board members behave in a boardroom and what we expect from our leaders.

Board membership has, comparatively recently, moved from an all-male activity to one that involves women.

Generational differences surface as the Depression generation interacts with Baby Boomers and Busters.

International organizations are served by boards whose members are of a variety of nationalities and languages.

These differences can be a bane or a blessing. They can pull the board to its lowest common denominator, or they may draw the best from each member, producing a truly powerful dynamic. There are at least four practices a diverse board can undertake to bring about a positive corporate culture:

- Consciously recognize the differences in its ranks and seek to understand them with an open mind;
- Create opportunities and allow the time for diverse directors to become personally acquainted;
- Cultivate an atmosphere of open-mindedness, tolerance, and respect;
- Keep focused on a shared vision, driving differences into insignificance.

Serving

"On Your Behalf"

Directors hold others accountable, but they, too, are accountable. They are trustees and, as such, are expected to produce the ends for which the organization exists. Their accountability is both legal and moral.

Director accountability expresses itself in a variety of ways. In community based organizations, such as a private school or hospital, directors know who elected them and understand generally what members expect. They know their actions are subject to scrutiny—when they make controversial decisions, they hear about it.

Directors of national or international organizations are, by comparison, remote from their membership. Members of such organizations cannot speak with a united voice. Their boards are usually self-perpetuating, meaning that directors, not members, fill board vacancies.

In either case, directors need to remember that their particular organization exists for a purpose. A director's first duty is to understand what that is, and to make every effort to produce it. Often the purpose is an activity individual members cannot do by themselves. Boards which become disconnected from, or indifferent to, their members' wishes are on slippery ground.

Understanding what members want begins best with a servanthood attitude, such as, "We serve on your behalf." Wise directors have their antennae out. They ask open questions, and, when asked to explain themselves, they respond in a non-defensive way. ("Amazing what you can learn by looking around!")

The best reading of what members want is to note what they support. When members fail to support an activity, it signals that either they have not understood what is being attempted, or they are not in favor of it. Contributors vote with their pocketbooks. Fund-raisers know that fund-raising is first about building relationships and communicating with members, and second about money.

A third way boards read their members' wishes is by doing a survey or commissioning a membership profile. Are you appealing to soccer moms or the AARP crowd? Are you representing church people or service-club types? One organization I know made major changes when they learned that their biggest giver group was women over 70 years of age. When organizations misread their membership, their fund-raising return on investment is poor and their future is uncertain.

Legally, directors owe "care, loyalty, and obedience" to organizations they serve. They are required to perform their duties with the care exercised by ordinarily prudent persons. Directors are expected to act in the best interest of the organization and are prohibited from furthering their private interests. Their good faith should never be in question.

Directors of public charities should be humbled by the trust placed in them. They should be able to face their members and say, "We are serving on your behalf. We are performing our duties faithfully, conscientiously, and to the best of our abilities." Directors can do no more. They should do no less.

Decision-Making

Decision-making is an essential board function. Remove decision-making from a board's duties and the reason for having a board disappears. When boards fail to make decisions, the organization is left to drift. The result is a vacuum and confusion.

Yet many boards go to great lengths to avoid making decisions, and they actually succeed! One board I served on made at most one, maybe two, basic decisions in a three-year period. "Who," I asked myself, "is making decisions? Or is nothing happening?"

Boards are rightfully judged by the decisions they make. Examine your minute book for the past year or five years. Organizations without fail approve minutes and reports "with appreciation," but what more do they do? What decisions do they make?

Some decisions are the board's responsibility. They cannot be delegated. Minimally, boards must establish the purposes for which the organization exists. They set the context and the parameters within which other decisions are made. A board approves an annual plan and budget which state, in broad terms, how effort and money will be allocated. Boards make policies, which are basically instructions for the future. Boards that fail to make these basic decisions abdicate their role.

Some boards are busy making decisions, but they are the wrong decisions. Directors should ask themselves regularly, "Is this our decision to make, or should it be delegated?"

Another question boards should ask is, "Is this issue ready for a decision? Has it been properly examined? Have the necessary people been consulted?" Many decisions are easily made after facts involved have been thoroughly and systematically researched and properly laid out in a well-written proposal.

Still another necessary inquiry boards ought to make of themselves is, "Are we making *good* decisions?" Many decisions are relatively inconsequential and can be easily reversed. Others are truly the proverbial fork in the road. Consequences may be greatly divergent and permanent.

Decisions test a board's ability to discern. "Is this a really great idea, or is it a huge distraction? Will it further our mission?" Boards tend to act cautiously, but wisdom is not always on the side of caution.

Nonprofit boards must learn better how to take *calculated risks,* while minimizing risk. Clumsy decision-making assumes more risk than is necessary.

Intuition should not be denied in the decision-making process. It may be subconscious wisdom. Not everything can be reduced to formulas. When my heart arrives at a different conclusion than my head, I hesitate, although I must also allow for the cowardice factor. Some people are always faint of heart. They never find the right circumstance in which to step outside the status quo. Boards that perpetually opt for half a loaf, or wait for yet another fact, miss the window of opportunity.

Dipping Too Deep?

All boards face a common temptation—spending too much time on administrative detail. They tend to control instead of lead. From where does this obsession come, this bad habit which is so hard to break? The tendency has its roots in some powerful dynamics which must be understood before they can be corrected.

First, most directors function below the line in "real life." (See diagram on page 6). Many are CEOs or managers. Their natural tendency is to think *how* something should be done, when, in their board capacity, they should be addressing *what* is to be done. Many rose through the ranks by their attention to detail. Now they are expected to concentrate on the big picture. They are accustomed to having a wrench on every nut. In their board role they have no wrench. Making the transition from below-the-line to above-the-line-thinking is like asking a right-handed person to write left-handed. It does not come naturally. It requires practice and discipline.

The tendency to dip deep is exacerbated by the fact that above-the-line board work is abstract, whereas below-the-line administrative work is, by comparison, concrete. The former has to do with ideas, the latter with activities. Board work is head work; it can be done without hands. Administrative work involves both hands and head. When left to do what comes naturally, many directors are naturally drawn below the line.

Contributing to this tendency is the fact that in young organizations this division of functions is not as pronounced. Directors get into the habit of doing below-the-line work and enjoy it. They resist making the transition to undertaking governance as the organization matures, and in so doing eventually retard its development.

Dipping too deep has at least four negative consequences. One, it overloads the board. Directors get exhausted, burned out below the line. Two, having expended their energy below the line, directors have insufficient energy and time to do their above-the-line governance work. Three, excessive director involvement below the line tends to confuse staff about its role. This demoralizes staff, particularly if governance work is being neglected. Finally, seeing that governance work is not getting done, or is being done haphazardly, staff moves into the vacuum, leading to conflict with the board. This completes a cycle in which no one is doing what they are supposed to do.

This unfortunate tendency can only be corrected when boards make a greater and more consistent effort to concentrate on their governance role. Only after the board is clear about its role can the rest of the persons in the organization be clear about their roles.

The tendency to dip too deep is lessened when boards do their work increasingly by establishing board-approved policies. Policy statements summarize what the board wants to say on a given subject, freeing the staff to proceed with implementation. Having delegated a task with instructions (policies), the board can back away and let the process work. The board observes, but it does not micromanage. It can and should check that the organization's mission is being accomplished, but it does not interfere or second-guess.

Good organizations, in short, have a clear division of responsibilities between board and staff, which is understood and respected by both. Each has confidence and trust in the other, resulting in mutual respect and goodwill.

Vision

Who needs it?

Vision is needed only by directors who are concerned about the future. Others don't need to bother. Pessimists and fatalists don't need vision. They believe what will be will be. "Sufficient unto the day is the evil thereof." "Why borrow trouble by trying to anticipate tomorrow if you can barely cope with today?"

This essay is for directors who believe they can and should, within reason, plan their organization's future. Planning and visioning are related but different. Vision has to do with imagining what you want to become, what you want to achieve, but what is now beyond reach.

Planning makes vision a reality. It puts wheels on the dream. It projects a sequence for what needs to be done and assigns responsibilities for realizing the dream.

Boards do not deliberately decide to ignore visioning or planning. More often their lack of attention to this area comes as the result of too many other preoccupations. Meetings begin with housekeeping—minutes, reporting, formalities. I believe in taking care of housekeeping—it is necessary—but unless boards get beyond housekeeping, the house collapses.

The time comes when boards must put business-as-usual aside to address the future strategically, when they must ignore the urgent to be able to address the important. Exercising vision requires a board to lift itself out of the present and to project itself vicariously into the future. Only by thinking strategically are organizations able to get outside the boxes which constrain them.

Many complain that change is so sudden and relentless. We convince ourselves that the future sneaks up on us, catching us unaware, as though it were some conspiracy. Not true. We ignore signs that things are changing, until suddenly, a tidal wave of deferred change hits us, and we are overwhelmed.

Strategic planning begins by freeing ourselves from the present and peering into the future. In this process boards ask themselves, where are we vulnerable? What is winding down, wearing out, about to become obsolete? What new opportunities await us? What is waiting to be born?

Visioning may be likened to seeing in the dark. Only after the eye has adjusted to the darkness is it able to detect a beam of light and, eventually, the outline of objects in a dark room. Similarly, until the mind's eye is released from everyday routine, it is unable to see what is not yet, but could be.

Boards like to fix things. They should also spend time prospecting . . . imagining the future and reflecting this in their planning. Before someone can make a rose garden, she must be able to imagine one. Boards perpetually complain about financial constraints. The truth is that most organizations are funded at about the level of their vision. Before they need substantially more money, they need more vision.

The Bible has it right: "Where there is no vision, the people perish."

Committees

Church and nonprofit organizations do much of their work through committees. They see them as indispensable. Many boards require each director to serve on at least one standing committee. In many boards, committee work takes up as much time as board meetings themselves. It is important, therefore, that boards get good results from the time invested in committees.

When John Carver, the organizational guru, was asked how many committees the ideal board should have, his surprising answer was none! None? That sounds like heresy to board leaders who think the appointment of many committees is proof that much good work is getting done. That may not be the case.

For all the good they do, committees are not a cure-all. Unless precautions are taken, committees can be a colossal waste of time. The correct response by an overworked board—and don't most boards feel overworked?—is not necessarily to appoint another committee.

Committees, at their worst, compromise matters to the lowest common denominator. They slow things down. They kill more ideas by their cautious scrutiny than they generate. An experienced administrator, reflecting on his most worthy accomplishments, admitted ruefully that many would have died in committee. "Committee meetings," a cynic has said, "is where you keep minutes and lose hours."

A committee is a gift when it gives in-depth study to an issue, arrives at a sound conclusion, and recommends it to the board in such a clear and convincing manner that the board does not feel the need to re-do its work.

Committees are subordinate to the board. They have only the authority given to them by the board. All committees should have a written job description which clearly states their authority and responsibility. Committees, too, need an annual work plan which identifies the issues they will address. They are expected to keep detailed minutes and keep the board well informed of their activities.

Peter Drucker observes that high performance organizations make extensive use of special committees, sometimes called task groups or teams, to address important issues. Such committees are given a memo of assignment which states what they are expected to accomplish, by when, and in what form. When the committee has completed its assignment, it is thanked and dissolved.

To restrain the tendency to appoint committees whimsically (a board I know has 17 and still feels overworked), I suggest a minimalist position. No more committees than necessary, no bigger than necessary (a good committee can consist of two members), meeting no more often and no longer than necessary. Teleconferencing can be used to good advantage if good procedures are followed.

Committees are not an end in themselves. They are a means to an end, that end being to aid the board in the fulfillment of its mission.

Improving
Director Effectiveness

When directors are elected to a board, they are honored, even humbled. They want to be of service. Over time an attitude of possessiveness emerges for many. Though they wouldn't say so, they begin to believe, "This chair belongs to me." They begin to see reelection as a right.

There are strong reasons favoring long tenure. One is the benefit of experience. Experience is valuable, to be sure, but unless it is balanced with vision the organization ossifies.

Feelings are a major factor. No one relishes the thought of informing faithful, long-term board members that their services are no longer needed. The easy way out is to re-nominate them regardless of their contributions.

The difficulty some organizations have in recruiting new directors contributes to the problem. Before long, such organizations become captive to their senior members. How do boards balance the need for new blood with the value of experience?

Boards can do at least four things to bring about improvement in this vital area:

1. Stop perpetuating the notion that election is for life. Reelection should not be regarded as automatic. It must be earned by the quality of service rendered.

2. Evaluation: Some boards use a system of peer review. Others use a self-assessment procedure. Both suggest that directors should have goals for what they want to accomplish.

3. Term and/or age limits: They are arbitrary, to be sure. Under some circumstances they are the best of imperfect options. Directors should know they have a limited time within which to make their contributions; then it is someone else's

turn. Most directors have given their best by the time they have served three three-year terms.

4. In wrestling with the issue I have developed a fourth option with attractive features, although not all boards have the courage and discipline to adopt it. Boards routinely require all directors to resign upon completion of five or six years of service. In their letters of resignation board members give assurance of their continued support and goodwill. They may, if they wish, volunteer their willingness to serve another term, but they know that is at the discretion of the electors, without obligation. This leaves the electors free to decide what will serve the organization best.

Simultaneously, boards need a procedure to recruit strong replacements and to provide for in-service training. The goal of every board should be to elect the best qualified persons available, and then to make them even better through experience and training. Training enriches a director and makes recruitment easier. Dynamic organizations have a waiting list of directors available to serve when an opening occurs.

Effective organizations are led by effective boards, made up of effective people. Organizations seldom rise above the competencies of those who direct them. Healthy organizations provide for the infusion of new blood, which, when blended with the continuity provided by continuing directors, produces a powerful dynamic. Directors should have a vision for the future, including what their own contributions might be. Dynamic boards have no free-ride seats.

Professionals in the Boardroom

One bonus of board service is the friends you make and the fine people you meet. Board service is a magnet that selects persons of generous spirit. (That is not to deny that selfishness does creep in at points.) We all bring what we have and know and give ourselves to a cause we believe in. This includes professionals—physicians, lawyers, teachers—and business persons. Professionals, however, have a special challenge, which is the subject of this essay.

Professionals grow accustomed to operating from the respect their hard-earned credentials afford them. They bring with them the self-confidence and, on occasion, the arrogance of the field in which they have distinguished themselves. They do not always recognize that professionals outside their field of expertise are amateurs. Not only are they amateurs, they can be *dangerous* amateurs, for two reasons:

First, they are saddled with over-confidence. Physicians as a group, for example, have the reputation of making poor investments. Their expertise in medicine does not carry over into the field of investing. But because they have earned competence in one field, they assume, to their sorrow, it applies also where it has not been earned.

Second, it is common for others to confer on professionals expertise they have not earned, and, therefore, to expect a level of performance they cannot always produce. It is sad and sobering to see someone flounder or fail, often for reasons they themselves do not understand.

I have two purposes in pointing out the awkward situation: first, to caution professionals to be fair with themselves. They should be aware that they are operating outside their expertise and should discipline themselves to be in a learning mode. They will be most effective if they make their contribution with respect for the wisdom of others and the group.

Equally, my purpose is to suggest that others refrain from loading professionals down with expectations they have not earned and which, in most cases, they have not requested. Do not automatically assume that because she is an attorney, or because he is a successful business person, she or he should serve as chairperson. The best chairperson is not necessarily one who knows law or can manage a large corporation, but one who draws wisdom from the group.

This also explains why I prefer not to use honorary or professional titles in the boardroom. Those titles have been earned and apply in another setting. The playing field in the boardroom is level.

When we invited Richard Celeste, former governor of Ohio, to join the board of Habitat For Humanity International, we suggested, somewhat hesitatingly, that he would be expected to leave his titles and (neck) ties at home. Had we known him better we would have known the concern was unnecessary. He blended into the Habitat culture beautifully, but that is not always the case.

There are no professionals in the boardroom because board service is not a profession. We are all amateurs trying to do our little bit, learning as we go.

Boardroom Bullies

Board work is, by definition, teamwork. Persons who join a board are expected to surrender their personal agenda in favor of a collective process, for the common good.

But it doesn't always happen. There are board members who usurp their role as directors. Through charisma or arrogance, and with the acquiescence of a silent majority, they seize power which exceeds what was intended. In a word, they become a menace in what is meant to be a democratic arena. What can be done about it?

First, it is good to be reminded that the chair is responsible for how the board functions. Chairs must exercise control of the meeting and board dynamic. If a problem arises which goes beyond what can appropriately be dealt with in an open session, the chair should meet with the offender privately. This is without doubt among the least cherished of roles assigned to the chair, but becomes necessary on occasion. Chairs must be willing to put the prestige and power of their office on the line to avoid making a ruse out of the board process.

But chairs can't do it alone, and sometimes the chair is the culprit. The first thing every board member is obligated to do is to vote his/her conscience. Many directors grouse in the corridor, but vote in whatever direction the momentum seems to be going. They deserve what they get. Directors must exercise their authority. Bully behavior must be confronted; otherwise it becomes an uncontrolled menace.

The annual board evaluation session is another place to address inappropriate behavior. In this session a board should analyze how it functions as a collective body. Is the board good at addressing a variety of issues, allowing for differing points of view, and finally arriving at a wise conclusion? Do a few members dominate while the rest give their passive consent? Can the quiet voices be heard? Sometimes directors don't know how they are being perceived. Sometimes they speak because others don't. This in turn causes others not to speak, with the result that the problem feeds on itself.

It is a sad contradiction that bully directors frequently get re-elected by persons they have intimidated, and who resent them. The performance of a new director cannot be predicted with certainty, but if a director shows bully tendencies, and if efforts to re-direct such an individual do not succeed, that person should not be re-elected. Such situations should be handled in the nomination process, sensitively but decisively. Rehabilitation is always the preferred option, but non-election is a last resort.

Board work is not for everyone. I have known very intelligent and dedicated persons who never became good directors. Temperament and training have a lot to do with it. One person I was acquainted with had gotten a bad reputation on a board. Everyone was frustrated, including the offender. In desperation he was removed from all boards. After a period of tension and re-grouping everyone involved agreed it had been the right thing to do.

Staff-Driven

Good or Bad?

Most issues come to the board through staff. Staff must continually decide what is within its authority to act upon and what needs to be brought to the board and in what form. When staff retain too many prerogatives to themselves, they are accused of circumventing the board, and the organization inherits the reputation of being staff-driven. Is that bad?

Not necessarily. Bad is when no one is driving. Bad is when a board resents initiatives which staff originate and, instead of directing them, seeks to stifle them. Bad is when staff seek to circumvent rather than facilitate a board's rightful role. Bad is when staff, either out of timidity or incompetence, bring everything to the board indiscriminately, overloading the board and diminishing itself.

Good boards know their role and welcome staff initiatives. Instead of being resentful, they seek to get ahead of the curve. They do this be evaluating a new initiative objectively and then moving it onto the decision-making track.

John Carver, author and organizational mastermind, uses a set of mixing bowls as an illustration. The board, says Carver, is the big bowl. It makes the all-encompassing decisions.

The principal of a private school, for example, reports that there is interest in starting a preschool class. Instead of resenting the initiative and stating reasons why it shouldn't even be considered, the wise board asks if this is within its vision and mission. If so, it authorizes a feasibility process which also includes an enrollment and cost projection. Returning to the big bowl illustration, the board establishes the parameters within which the process may proceed.

The administrative staff is in charge of a second bowl which, in this illustration, is a feasibility study that is informed by the parameters established by the board. A division of labor is operating which permits and provides for the participation of both the board and staff. Instead of resenting each other, they act as partners.

Not only must staff learn what to bring to the board, it must become skillful at how and when. To continue the preschool illustration, it would be folly to bring an ambitious proposal to a meeting dominated by a financial crisis. The presenter should have some sense of how the board will want to proceed. The presentation should anticipate questions the board will ask and should have, at least, initial answers. While those making the presentation should not expect carte blanch approval on the first round, their recommendation should be in the realm of what the board is likely to approve.

Some feel that when a board sets parameters for staff it is being too confining. I believe it is helpful for a board to set parameters within which a process may proceed. The more pertinent question is if the bowl size they have drawn is appropriate. If the bowl is too small, it stifles initiative. If it is too large, it does not define the context adequately. The secret is finding a bowl of the right size.

Trust

Trust. Organizations can't function without it. Much organizational activity takes place behind the scenes. The public, or even the membership, does not know what goes on in board meetings. School board directors can't know what goes on in the classroom. Hospital board directors can't be a secret eye on the ward. Directors of an international agency are far removed from the scene of action. Directors approve plans and policies and they receive reports, but beyond that they must trust those to whom they have delegated responsibility.

Trust is predicated on two things. The first is competence. Do they know what they are doing? The surgeon may have the best intentions, but unless he is competent, he does not merit trust.

Trust is also predicated on integrity. Is she trustworthy? Can I trust what she says? Is her "yes, yes," and her "no, no"? Does she say one thing in one setting and something else in another?

To be considered trustworthy, directors must both demonstrate their competence to do the right thing and establish their integrity. They must show that they will act in good faith.

The public will forgive an honest mistake, if it is convinced that those involved acted in good faith. But to violate the public trust is a serious offense which is long remembered. It erodes confidence, which erodes trust. This is illustrated by the crisis of confidence experienced by the United Way following the 1991 Aramany scandal.

Leaders of publicly supported organizations must establish that they are worthy of trust. Trust cannot be conferred. It is earned by performance over time. It is, ironically, often earned in a crisis. The trustworthiness of an individual or an organization is untested in ordinary times, but if leaders perform well under pressure, trust builds.

It seems unfair, and it is unfair, but trust that has been built up over many years can be lost in one bad incident. Reputation, both favorable and unfavorable, has a long tail. An organization may be highly regarded long after it is deserved, or it may take a long time to live down a bad mistake.

An organization's reputation makes people predisposed to trust or to distrust it. An organization with a sterling reputation can weather a storm because people believe in it; they trust it. Individuals or organizations who go into a crisis under suspicion do not get the benefit of the doubt.

This suggests that organizations must continually strive not only to do the right thing, but to build their public images. Unfortunately, this too can be carried to extremes. Image-building can become an obsession. Leaders who are overly concerned with image refuse to take risks. Their preoccupation becomes what looks good, rather than what is in the best long-term interests of the organization. They become the proverbial engine with a six-inch boiler and a six-foot whistle. Such an attitude and behavior undermine trust.

Trust is a test that healthy organizations must pass.

"The quality of its meetings
is a measure
of an organization's effectiveness.
Good organizations
have good meetings.
Good meetings, in turn,
make an organization better."

— from *Effective Meetings*

Meetings

Effective Meetings

Effective meetings do not begin with the gavel, but begin weeks, even months, before the meeting, when those responsible identify the agenda and make assignments.

A carefully prepared agenda is a prerequisite to an effective meeting. Meeting planners should place on the agenda only items which are ready for action. If the homework has not been done on an agenda item, boards should refuse to consider it. Doing so serves no good purpose. It is a waste of time. It can be harmful.

Every agenda item should be tested with the question, is this *board* business? Boards waste much time on issues which should never appear on their agenda. If a given item pertains to *means*, not *ends*, if it has to do with *how* something should be done rather than *whether* it should be done, the item is in doubt.

How issues are presented is of comparable importance. It is never appropriate to throw a provocative issue on the table and ask, "What shall we do?" A good presentation begins with a proposal which explains the background. Why is this on the agenda? To what problem is this the solution? What are we trying to correct? How? Who will do it? What will it cost? What will it accomplish? How will it be evaluated?

With this information in hand, preferably before the meeting, the board can go to work. It may, it should, probe. Then it should, without prolonged, inconclusive discussion, opt for one of the following options:
- Approve the proposal as presented.
- Approve it in amended form.
- Refer it for further study.
- Disapprove it.

If staff and committees are responsible to present reports and recommendations in advance of a meeting, board members are responsible to read, even study, these materials thoroughly. Too frequently board members place their meeting papers in a special file which they pick up on their way out of the office, intending to read them en route to the meeting. The speed of airplanes and the size of board books are a mismatch; too many directors arrive ill-prepared. This is inexcusable.

Coming well prepared does not mean, however, that directors should come with their minds firmly made up. That is to preclude the role of discussion. Board work is a collective process, drawing from the wisdom and experience of the gathered body. Directors should have their questions, even their reservations, in mind, but they should still be ready to listen to other points of view with open minds.

The role of the chair is obviously critical in the conduct of meetings. The chair should be involved in drafting the agenda. She is responsible to keep the discussion focused and moving toward a consensus. This goes better for me if I am not too invested in a predetermined outcome. The challenge facing every chair is to protect the bottom of the agenda, while being as unobtrusive as possible.

Let it not be said of you, as the Apostle Paul said to the Corinthians, "Your meetings do more harm than good." The quality of its meetings is a measure of an organization's effectiveness. Good organizations have good meetings. Good meetings, in turn, make an organization better.

Whose Rules of Order?

All public discourse is governed by rules. Formality general-ly increases in accordance with the number of persons participating. Over 100 years ago, Major Henry M. Robert wrote a book on parliamentary law. His starting point was the rules used in the British Parliament, adapted for use by the U.S. Congress. They have been revised so frequently that the title of the book has changed to *Robert's Rules of Order Revised*. These regulations are the universally accepted proce-dure by which business is transacted in a public setting.

Robert's Rules provide for an orderly, democratic process. They are based on the principle that the majority has the right to decide, the minority has a right to be heard, and the rights of absentees need to be protected. My 75th anniversary edition lists 44 motions and sets forth the use and functions of each.

With due respect for this revered authority, and, while affirming the need for order, my conclusion is that *Robert's Rules* are more appropriate in the U.S. Congress or in large assemblies, than for use by church and nonprofit committees and boards. In a less formal setting they are more likely to manipulate than to facilitate, to intimidate than to empower. They make me feel like David in Goliath's armor.

A good meeting is one in which members are free to address the issues and arrive at conclusions based on their collective experience and learning. In this process a synergistic effect emerges which transcends the wisdom contributed by any one member, or even the sum of the members. The strict enforce-ment of *Robert's* distracts from this kind of spontaneity.

Robert's has its place. Order there must be. But for church and nonprofit boards and committees, my preference is to min-imize legalism and simply to be informed by *Robert's*. As the

German proverb suggests, "This soup we will eat not as hot as it is cooked." The goal, instead, is to provide for and invite spontaneous but disciplined participation.

It is good to be reminded that although our system provides that "Majority rules," the majority is not always right. The Bible, in fact, likens the majority to the broad road that leads to destruction! And while the majority has its way, it still needs the support of the minority to make things work. Consensus is the ideal, but not always possible.

The test of a good meeting is not, did you conform to the letter of *Robert's Rules.* I am more inclined to ask, how well were Jesus' rules of love and justice practiced? Were the three principles under-girding *Robert's,* as summarized in paragraph two above, adhered to? Was there an open, trusting atmosphere where members expressed themselves freely and respectfully? Were good decisions made? Do they represent all who participated and are they owned by them?

When I transferred the Chair of Habitat for Humanity International to my successor, I gave him a towel representing a willingness to serve others, not a gavel; a Bible opened to I Corinthians 13, not *Robert's Rules of Order.*

The Role of the Chair

The role of the chair is the least defined and the least circumscribed role in the organization. The chair, many think, has the last word on every issue. Persons who have served in that capacity may dispute that, but that is the common interpretation and, in some settings, the expectation. As a chair I see myself facilitating the wishes of the members.

Leading a meeting is the chair's most visible task, and leading meetings is important. That is where boards do their work. Meetings should have a clear purpose. Why meet? That purpose should be consistent with the agenda, which is prepared by the chair in consultation with the CEO and board committees. Meeting planning should begin soon after the last meeting has adjourned. It involves identifying the issues to be addressed and making assignments needed to present the issues appropriately. The quality of a meeting is determined more by pre-meeting planning than by how it is conducted.

While a meeting is in process, the chair's role is to keep the discussion focused and to lead it to consensus. Only one issue can be examined at a time. If parallel issues are introduced, the chair is responsible to suggest the order in which the discussion will proceed. Allowing more than one issue on the floor leads to meeting merry-go-round, which eventually makes everybody unmerry. There is a time to "let the horses run," but meeting drift must be avoided.

Important as meeting performance is, the chair's equally important duty has to do with non-meeting functions. When the board is not in session, the chair speaks on its behalf. The chair is responsible to oversee and coordinate the work of board committees and to help them see their roles in the context of the whole organization.

The chair also serves as the CEO's supervisor. This suggests that they should meet regularly. Ideally the CEO finds in the chair a wise counselor with whom s/he is compatible. Minimally the two must trust and respect each other, and their relationship must be functional.

It is helpful to be reminded that the chair is responsible for how the board functions, while the CEO is responsible for how operations run. The CEO is responsible *to* the board, not *for* it. Both the chair and the CEO must be careful not to usurp the board's rightful role and to keep it well informed.

When directors misbehave, and they do occasionally, it is the chair's duty to bring them into line. This unpleasant task should never fall to the CEO, nor should a director's inappropriate conduct go unnoticed.

Chairs, too, need to accept their accountability. "No one, absolutely no one,"says Robert Greenleaf, "is to be entrusted with the operational use of power without the oversight of fully functioning trustees. The enemy to effective leadership is strong natural servants who have the potential to lead but do not lead, or who choose to follow a non-servant."

The Board Book

What may have started out as a file folder, containing the meeting agenda and perhaps a few reports, has in many organizations graduated to being a book, and I mean BOOK. A fellow director once asked jokingly if future board books might come equipped with wheels.

A board book for each board meeting is essential. It should contain the information a board needs to make good decisions. Selecting that material is more difficult than one might think. Most issues needing board action present themselves first to staff. Staff must decide what is within its authority and what must be referred to the board, and in what form. If staff keep a board busy with trivia, or if a board demands trivia, board work is trivial. On the other hand, if staff take upon themselves resolving issues which are rightfully in the board's province, they usurp the board's role. This is a balance every board and staff must strike.

Staff or committee members who bring the board a matter for review or action are responsible to help the board understand the background and practical implications of that issue. They should also present the board with options—preferably an actionable recommendation. Then the board must arrive at a decision. It is not enough to identify a problem. This background information should have been in the board book.

It is, by definition, impossible to have a good meeting with a poor board book. A poor board book is a distraction. It focuses attention on the wrong issues. This happens easily because the board book is assembled by *how* people (staff) for *what/why* people (board). Unless staff and board are able to work together at making the needed conversion, the board will be busy with what is essentially staff work. Boards need to know what is happening at the operational level, but their concentration must be on *what* is to be done. This is hard to do if the board book is written only from an administrative perspective.

Information which comes from executive levels within the organization is more likely to be useful for board work than that which comes from lower levels. This is not to diminish the good and essential work done at lower levels. It suggests that information from lower levels is usually more detailed than is useful for board purposes and is not sufficiently integrated with what is happening within the whole organization.

A good board book is easy to use. Pages are numbered and may be color-coded. A table of contents serves as a meeting map, identifying major action items. Afterthought handouts can cause confusion and should, therefore, be avoided.

What is the appropriate length of a board book? Board book writers should understand that more may not be better. Even good things can be overdone. Sometimes a fat board book suggests the inability of staff to choose priorities well or to fail to understand the board's role clearly. At the risk of being arbitrary, I find it hard to imagine circumstances which warrant more than 100 pages (I have seen 300.) Boards that meet monthly need substantially less.

To serve its purpose, a board book must be in the directors' hands at least two weeks before a meeting. Board books are worth the effort only if directors read and study them in advance.

Followership

Leaders are exalted. Everybody wants to be chief, captain, chairman, CEO, the lead dog. Leaders are the ones with six, and even seven, figure salaries. They get the ink.

My spell check accepts the word "leadership"; it rejects the word "followship." "Followship" is not a word. But there must be followers if there are to be leaders. As the words of the old song promised, "You can't have one without the other." Even as there are good and not-so-good leaders, the same is true of followers. Followership, too, must be learned.

There is a legend that if you hold a stick across the path of a herd of sheep, requiring them to jump before they can pass, and then remove the stick after the first three have jumped, the sheep that follow will still jump at that precise point. Is that the model I am advocating?

Followership is the ability to follow while still thinking for yourself. Your starting point is to be willing to follow, but not blindly. When your head tells you something is wrong, you must say so. You challenge the leader, while still regarding him/her as leader.

Some people are natural followers. They get in line. But a board made of that kind of sheep is incomplete. One person is thinking; the rest follow blindly. That is dangerous. It is denigrating to all but the leader. It isn't even good for the leader.

Followers sometimes see or feel things that elude the leader. Leaders are by definition out in front. They are in a certain kind of bubble. They get there first. Bold leaders try things that are unproven, and, because they are unproven, they need to be tested. It is hard to lead and test at the same time. Testing—asking, is this the right way?—is, therefore, a good role for followers, but only if they do it constructively.

This is the point at which followership skill is needed. Anyone can follow blindly. Anyone can second-guess. Anyone can be disruptive or contrary. *Skilled* followers take their cues from the leader. That is their starting point, but they do not take such cues without consideration. They think. And when they don't arrive at the same conclusions as the leader, they find constructive ways of saying so, and then participate in arriving at a better alternative.

"The best subordinate," an experienced supervisor once told me, "is not the one who always agrees. It most assuredly is not the one whose nature is always to resist. The best subordinate is the one who interacts with me in a manner that adds confidence to our decision-making process."

My son who works for a Fortune 500 company tells me that he never tells his boss something is impossible or even impractical. He helps the boss think through the implications of an order he has given, and this approach has, on occasion, caused him to change the order.

Consider the metaphor, "The strength of the wolf is in the pack; the strength of the pack is in the wolf." Good followers make good leaders better. Good leaders produce a better pack. Both leaders and followers need to be strong to produce a maximum effect.

Fostering Participation

The mood of the present era is to welcome increased participation. "Down with authoritarianism." "Flatten the pyramid." Servanthood leadership is experiencing a renaissance. The new words are Group and Team.

Having seen organizations riddled with domination and manipulation, I understand and hear the enthusiasm for greater participation. But everything has its downside, even something so noble as egalitarianism. The ambitious goal of this essay is to discuss the downside of the current trend, so we can enjoy its benefits while diminishing its downside.

Today the fear of being thought autocratic makes leaders reluctant to exercise leadership. The result is a vacuum in many organizational dynamics. There is still a place for the skillful leader who can, without employing strong-arm tactics, keep an organization off the shoals of indecision. Leadership is still needed to facilitate a group process. Despite our current preferences, the leadership styles we want to distance ourselves from accomplished things which are difficult, if not impossible, under the "reluctant-leadership" approach.

A leader from the old school, although by no means an ego-driven autocrat said, "The time comes when leaders must make the hard decision, and let the heathen rage." President Truman said, "The buck stops here."

Not all that passes for participatory leadership is driven by respect for the wisdom of the group and each individual in it. Some is plain timidity and lack of decisiveness and vision.

Participation carried to excess leads to a false sense of well-being. Just because a room full of enthusiasts arrive at a unanimous conclusion is no guarantee that it is a good one. To the contrary, boards which value consensus above all else find it hard to foster independent thinking. If, in a former age, directors acted on occasion as horses with blinders, the dynamic has shifted to one that can be likened to a flock of milling sheep.

It brings to mind what is referred to as The Abilene Syndrome. A group of friends, so the story goes, were bored in Abilene. One member suggested, "Let's go to—, a town some 60 miles away, where, I am told, they have excellent ribs." "Sounds good to me," chimed in a fun-loving member. Without further thought the group piled into an available car and were on their way. After 15 minutes, one member complained about the heat; the car had no AC and this was south Texas in summer. Then, it became clear, no one knew where the famous rib restaurant was located. Irritation became as apparent as the sweat on the friends' brows. When they finally found the restaurant, its service was slow and the ribs disappointing. One member's threshold had been reached. She blurted out, "Yeah, whose idea was this any way?" "Not mine," they chimed in one after another. They all participated in the decision, but no one was thinking clearly. The trip home was hot and long.

The challenge facing contemporary leaders is to lead without dominating, to invite participation that brings out the best ideas within the group, to be decisive without being impulsive. It is a daunting challenge, but it can be done. It is being done.

When Did You Last Vote Nay?

When did you last vote nay at a board meeting? Is it wrong to vote nay? Is it disruptive? Is it, perhaps, disloyal?

The truth is that some directors always vote in the affirmative. When turning the chair of a prominent church organization over to his successor, the long-time chairman said proudly that during his 33-year reign there had never been a dissenting vote; all actions had been unanimous. Really? Is that good or bad? (I learned later that when someone cast a dissenting vote, the revered chairman asked the dissenter to change her/his vote, making the action unanimous.)

The ayes have it, but they aren't always right. Nor do they necessarily represent the best collective thinking of the majority. Sometimes what is perceived to be the majority is actually the will of a powerful few, with the acquiescence of the rest.

Many directors, sadly, do not think for themselves. They become adept at sensing which way the wind is blowing and predictably vote with the majority. They lack confidence in their ability to represent what they believe. Not wanting to embarrass themselves, they take refuge in the majority.

Many board meetings are conducted in an atmosphere which seeks only agreement with what has been preordained. Intimidation squelches independent thinking. Out of the Watergate tragedy comes the quote, "To get along, you go along."

The mark of a good board and chair is that board members are encouraged to explore alternatives and exercise independent thinking. Good decision-making requires that all points of view are given due consideration.

In this process it is good to recognize the unique role of newly elected directors. Being new, freshman directors should be respectful of what has preceded them. The pity is, many stay in that dependent stance. They never mature to the point where they exercise independent judgment.

Some veteran directors are irritated when new directors question something which they think has been resolved long ago, or given up as impossible. Allowing this irritation to show is enough to intimidate many new directors. This is unfortunate since, in my experience, the call for re-examination is one of the most valuable functions new directors perform. The right to question something is necessary to save a board from falling into a closed-system syndrome. It is also needed to give new directors the freedom they need to mature as directors.

Not only is it permissible to vote nay, it is necessary on occasion. It need not be disruptive, nor should it be seen as disloyal. The ayes have it, but a nay vote is an indication that there is a point of view which the adopted proposal has not taken into account. It could prove to be valid.

Those on the short end of a vote should remember that they are obligated to support the majority action and help make it work.

Politics in the Boardroom

Politics in the boardroom? Incongruous? Incompatible with the spirit of selfless service commonly associated with church or nonprofit boards? Maybe.

"Politics," it is said, "is the art of the possible." In the best sense, it is lining up the ducks. Someone has an idea s/he wants the board to adopt. For this to happen s/he needs the support of at least half the board members. So s/he goes about selling the idea. What is wrong with that?

In the process of selling the idea s/he runs into fellow directors who, too, have some ideas for which they want support. This leads to a little quid pro quo. "Support me for chair and I'll get you appointed to the committee you want!" Now we are getting closer to the edge. But maybe not.

Boardroom politics are bad when they are used to circumvent the will of the majority. Our system of parliamentary law holds that the majority rules, right or wrong. When the cards are arranged to interfere with directors voting their best judgment on any issue, the democratic process is being corrupted.

Politics are bad when they are used to put self-interest above the good of the cause. Not only must nonprofit directors avoid personal gain, they must avoid the *appearance* of personal gain. Where their own self-interest is concerned, directors should handicap themselves.

Violations can occur at three levels of severity. Healthy boards should be able to cope with mild abuses. They are a nuisance and a warning but not unexpected in an imperfect world.

More severe abuses, which interfere with board objectivity and process, need to be dealt with by either or both the chair and board service committee. Following the principle that the chair is responsible for how the board functions, the chair must find a way to confront the issue with the least disruption possible. It should not be necessary for the CEO to get directly involved, nor would that be appropriate in our suggested separation of powers.

The board service committee can work on the issues either through the annual board evaluation or through director nominations. A board which allows a director involved in self-serving practices to be reelected, without addressing and correcting the situation, allows the problem to become more deeply entrenched.

If the problem is blatant and clear, it becomes a legal issue and must be dealt with in that way. Most bylaws give the organization the prerogative to terminate a director midterm for just cause. In rare and severe cases the process must be allowed to follow a legal procedure.

Prevention is the best strategy. If an organization's mission is clear and urgent, and if directors are carefully screened and their performance is reviewed and monitored, problems should not appear. If they do, they cannot be ignored or swept aside. They will not go way; they will only get worse. Once a problem become endemic, it threatens the whole organization.

Politics in the boardroom? A warning at best; a sign of serious trouble at worst.

Transparency

Healthy organizations operate with an attitude of openness. Their leaders are prepared to explain their actions. They know and accept that public scrutiny goes with the territory. They use no smoke nor mirrors.

Were I, by way of contrast, to imagine an organization in Hell, I would find *manipulated* information. There would be many cliques and many rumors and much subterfuge and deceit. Everything would be shrouded in secrecy. Feeding into that insecure environment would be a steady flow of information, not all of which would be true. Leaders would continually go to great lengths to foster a sterling public image. The confusion and distrust would become so great that the enterprise would soon disintegrate.

Confidentiality has its place. Not everybody is entitled to know everything. Some information and files should not be widely available. But healthy organizations keep the list of privileged information short. They practice the discipline of operating in an open room.

It is appropriate on occasion to ask someone to leave the room, but not when the reasons for doing so are cowardice and deceit. The standard of reliability of what is said, I have observed, has a tendency to drop when the doors close. Closed doors give too easy license to speculation, which often goes far beyond established facts. I have witnessed scenes which were not only unhelpful; they were unquestioningly harmful. I find myself wondering if something should be said if it can't be said in the presence of the person under discussion.

I still support the need for boards to have executive sessions, but I do so with reservation and with a call for greater discipline for members and the chair.

When the doors open again, the person(s) who were excluded from the discussion still need to be dealt with. A decision has presumably been reached in their absence. Questions have been raised. Suspicions have been aroused. The person(s) who were the subject of the discussion are affected by something from which they were deliberately excluded. They should not be left to twist slowly in the wind. Minimally, they deserve a prompt and thorough summary of what was decided and why. This should be done, preferably, before the meeting adjourns, or soon thereafter.

Challenging directors to operate in an open room is not imposing a handicap on them. To the contrary, it is asking them to work in a way which will serve them—and the organization—better in the long run.

Directors of nonprofit organizations need to remember that they have accepted a public trust. That fact carries with it an expectation of transparency which exceeds the standard demanded of a private effort. Only those willing to operate within this open atmosphere should accept the call to public service.

Enough!

He was angry. Not furious, but clearly out of patience. "This discussion has gone on long enough, it is not going anywhere, and I am not pleased with the direction we're taking!"

It was the second day of a meeting. We were trying to find agreement on a vision statement. The members were exhausted. Some were eyeing the clock with their departure times in mind. A good statement had been put forward and promptly shot down. A few more attempts were made, and then we settled down to wordsmithing. Back and forth, up and down—like a beginners' soccer match played at midfield. It looked as though we would adjourn without reaching agreement on a statement.

Then one director had sense enough to cry, "Enough!" When asked to offer his suggestion, he sputtered a bit and then came up with something akin to the statement the group had rejected an hour earlier. "Christ's servants, freeing the world from leprosy." There were a few moments of quiet reflection, and then, one after another, the weary directors nodded agreement. "That's it." No motion was needed. Consensus had been found.

The moral of the story is there comes a time when enough is enough. Some directors don't know when to stop. Some like to hear themselves speak, whether or not what they are saying makes sense. Chairs, particularly those committed to an open, democratic process, hesitate to cut anybody off. So who is willing to risk calling the question, choking off further debate?

Sometimes, as happened above, it is best done by a board member, someone other than the chair. But that is a risk. Maybe the majority want to continue what you think is a circular exercise. Yet even the turtle makes progress only when sticking out its head. Effective boardsmanship requires someone to stick out her/his neck, but to do so appropriately and sensitively.

In situations like this, be careful not to tie yourself too firmly to what you are suggesting. By that I mean, allow the group to reject what you are saying without turning on you. In this illustration, there was no mistaking this director's frustration. His patience had been exhausted. Had he blown his whistle 15 minutes sooner, it would have been disruptive, and the group might well have elected to continue debate. Had he done it 30 minutes later, the collective feelings of frustration might have reached a point where directors had begun to excuse themselves from the room. Had he coupled his motion with some tasteless, personal remarks, implicating others in the room, the group mood might have turned on *him*, causing him to lose face. Wisely, he did it just right, and we respected him for it.

"Christ's servants, freeing the world from leprosy" the mission statement became. A good process had produced a good result.

"The next time
staff present your board
with an impressive list of activities,
ask in a simple and sincere way,
'So what?'
What difference did it/will it make?
Board work
is about outcomes,
not about activities."

— from *Activities vs. Outcomes*

The
Bigger Picture

Entrepreneurial or Bureaucratic

An entrepreneurial spirit is willing to assume risk to achieve an objective. It is bold and creative. That stands in contrast to a bureaucratic spirit which is inclined to follow a routine in a mechanical, prescribed way. All organizations operate somewhere on this continuum.

Most organizations, in fact, begin entrepreneurially. Someone has an idea which s/he thinks will revolutionize the world. The entrepreneur is willing to assume the risk which is part of a new venture.

As organizations mature they have more to protect and to conserve. They have less room for experimentation and error. The tendency is for organizations to get more conservative as they become more established. Those who function within them begin to operate more bureaucratically. More stringent procedures are introduced. The number and size of manuals increase. The focus becomes doing things right.

To stay alive, to stay relevant in a rapidly changing world, organizations need to maintain an entrepreneurial spirit. One organization which illustrates this is Habitat for Humanity International. Founded by Millard Fuller, a lawyer, but an entrepreneur par excellence, Habitat started with a poignant idea— a simple house for everyone. The idea spread like wildfire, first in the South, then up the East Coast, through the Midwest, and down the West Coast. It took hold in country after country, until today there is a Habitat within reach of most people in the United States and Canada and in some 60 other countries. The combined budgets of the 1,500 Habitat affiliates have increased from thousands to millions, and now to billions. The creative, energetic spirit of Millard Fuller never rests. Like a heat-seeking laser, it keeps searching for new opportunities.

As Habitat began, Fuller called into being a board of directors and an administrative apparatus. The growing bureaucracy has overflowed building after building. It continually threatens to get out of hand—bureaucracies will do that—but it is needed. Without an administrative structure, the venture would surely disintegrate. But it is the entrepreneurial spirit which continues to blaze the trail.

Bureaucracies want to slow things down. They want to make activities neat and orderly by conforming to stringent procedures. That impulse has its place. The entrepreneurial spirit is supported and, at the same time, held in check by the bureaucracy. But the entrepreneur wants to be free to pursue new opportunities. When bureaucrats have full sway, everything is orderly but moving toward obsolescence. When entrepreneurs are allowed to operate unchecked, there is excitement in the air, but things get messy and out of control. The two need each other like a hammer needs nails.

Many directors are entrepreneurs in their work life. They take risks. Boards, particularly boards of successful ventures, are perpetually afraid of doing something which will endanger what has been won. They tend to become increasingly bureaucratic. Instead of looking through the telescope they orient themselves around the rearview mirror.

Boards are prone to opt for caution, but wisdom is not always on the side of caution. In the biblical story of the talents, the cautious person—for our purposes, the bureaucrat—was the loser. Caution has its place, but must be counterbalanced with vision and drive.

Money Matters

"**M**oney isn't everything, but it sure beats whatever is in second place." This little proverb, spoken by a consummate treasurer, may not capture the whole truth, but it has a corner of it. Surely money isn't everything, but not having enough money is also a problem. If it is hard to live with money, try living without it.

Nonprofit leaders are often accused of being lax with money. A consensus-building exercise I participated in asked us to produce an imaginary brochure. To understand the context better, one member asked, "Is it a nonprofit or a for-profit agency?" "What difference does it make? A brochure is a brochure," came the response. The tongue-in-cheek reply was, "Oh, if it is a nonprofit we don't need to worry about a budget. They just pay what it takes."

Some nonprofits operate that way.

In contrast, I once overheard a manufacturing executive and his head engineer talking as they redesigned a product they were planning to mass-produce. By eliminating one brace they saved 42 cents per unit. Now they were looking for ways to avoid an offsetting 25-cent increase. I asked myself, "When have I seen nonprofit executives work with that kind of sharp-pencil mentality?'

Many nonprofit leaders fall into a syndrome that assumes that if they had 50 percent more money their problems would disappear. The truth is many agencies don't know how to manage well the money they have. Nonprofits must continually be on guard against two kinds of waste.

The first is waste from inefficiency, from not doing heads-up business or from buying pencils from the wrong vendor. A man with executive experience in both the business and nonprofit worlds used to ask supervisors, "Do you have enough employees?" If the reply was yes, his response was, "Then you have one too many." The truth is that many nonprofits are far too comfortable—or far too busy with wrong things. A few dollars here and a few dollars there—they all add up and become part of a culture of indifference.

The bigger waste comes from tolerating an atmosphere of sloth and entropy. In a closed system, entropy increases, and energy available for productive activity decreases. The leader's first challenge is to arrest the natural forces which produce entropy. For nonprofit leaders that means being ready to let go of old, tired programs and being prepared to make room for new, vibrant programs.

When vision and mission are bold and compelling, they infuse energy into the system and all those in it. Millard Fuller, founder of Habitat for Humanity, once said, "When you get the vision right, it just soars!" The inverse is also true. When vision is lax, everything becomes limp and optional.

The business community is driven by the profit motive. What is the nonprofit equivalent?

Activities vs. Outcomes

Staff members can impress their boards with the numbers and kinds of activities they have underway. Their news releases boastingly tell about inputs. So many workers, so many tons, and so many hours. Boards love it. Directors are left with the impression that something is being accomplished. Maybe. Maybe not. The read question is what are the outcomes?

If you are running a school, how well are the graduates doing? What is your student retention rate? If you are ridding the world of leprosy how many cases did you find and cure? If you are running a camping program, how well were the campers served? If you are helping poor people afford decent houses, how many families succeeded in buying a good place to live?

Board work is not primarily concerned with keeping people busy. People will be busy all right, if not with important work, then with trivia. Boards are responsible to ensure that something is *accomplished*.

Boards must train their staffs that they will not be satisfied with a long and impressive list of activities. Activities are not the desired end. Activities are a *means* to an end. The end is those outcomes by which an organization's mission and vision are realized.

Many boards are unclear about the outcomes they desire because they are unclear about their mission. They aren't sure about their reasons for existing. They are so busy monitoring activities, they have lost sight of what it is they are meant to accomplish.

Call it reverse engineering. Instead of doing what they have always been doing, and even seeking to do it better, directors should be asking, what do we want to accomplish? They should then measure performance against that predetermined goal.

A freshman director of a respected Bible-translation mission noted that some translations were abandoned unfinished. When his observation was met with a defensive response, he asked firmly but politely that staff research how many translations had never been completed for any reason—illness, civil war, whatever. The findings surprised everyone. The organization acted to shorten the time required to complete a translation by using more computers. More stringent criteria for beginning a translation were adopted. The result was a noticeable improvement in performance, all because one director looked beyond input and insisted on knowing the outcome.

Evaluation is an essential requirement of outcome-based programming. Is something being served by our activities, or are we mostly fanning the air? Left-brained people are sometimes scorned for being too numbers-conscious. Statistics can be overdone, and not everything is quantifiable, but numbers do measure progress.

The next time staff present your board with an impressive list of activities, ask in a simple and sincere way, "So what?" What difference did it/will it make? Board work is about outcomes, not about activities.

Knowing (from Reporting)

Directors need to know what is going on. It is the board's business to know. Ignorance is no excuse. It is obvious, at the same time, that directors can't know everything, nor do they need to know everything. But they do need to know what is of essence. Never should a board be in the dark or taken by surprise. Directors own the bad with the good.

Directors are responsible to specify the information they need to do their work. Staff, the CEO in particular, are responsible to produce without fail what the board prescribes. Good reports not only anticipate questions, they answer them before they are asked. Good reports are:

- Informational—factual, they track the annual work plan.
- Analytical—they permit comparisons with previous years or industry standards.
- Concise—they are condensed to the basics.
- Reliable—they do not embellish.
- Explicit—they state what action is expected.

Reports should ideally be designed to serve a dual role. While giving the board information it needs, reports should help management with lateral communication and administrative tracking. A board can insure that subjects of special interest get tracked by requiring that they be included in reports.

While allowing that reporting must be adapted to the needs of each organization, the following schedule serves as a general model, especially for an organization with a scattered membership, whose board meets quarterly or semi-annually.

Within the first three working days of the month, the CEO prepares a one-page report summarizing the main activities and developments, both past and anticipated. To this is attached the monthly financial statement (cash flow) with a three-year comparison. The whole report consists of two sheets that required approximately three hours of staff time to prepare.

A more detailed report is prepared in each of the four quarters, with the fourth quarter serving also as the annual report. This is done under the direction of the CEO, with the participation of department heads. Whereas the monthly report is for information purposes only—no action is expected on the basis of these reports—the quarterly reports may be the basis for corrective action.

The most thorough analysis is reserved for the annual report, which is also the basis for the next year's planning.

Routine reports should be mailed to the board before the meeting, with limited opportunity for questions and discussion at the meeting. Directors are responsible to probe what is on the line and between the lines. They should be both analytical and intuitive. Even the hint of dishonest or misleading reporting cannot be tolerated. Directors are responsible to act on what they know.

Important as reporting is, it must not be permitted to take on a life of its own. Many boards yield the best hour of their meeting to reporting, leaving them with insufficient time to attend to other responsibilities. Reporting can be excessive, taking too much valuable time and adding to staff's workload. Reporting is not an end. It is the *means* to an end. That end is to help a board make decisions which will further its mission.

"We Had No Choice"

Did you ever hear, "We had no choice"? The statement is more likely an excuse than the imperative it is perceived to be. Boards have choices. They resort to this line when they want to escape responsibility for a decision they have made which they are unable to justify rationally. They do it when they are so locked into a line of thinking that they are incapable of considering other options.

The last time I heard this argument was when an organization felt pushed by competition into a new activity which was outside its competence. It allowed itself to accept a mandate which was, in fact, not a viable option. By being convinced that "they had no choice," they were ducking responsibility for the consequences. They killed debate. They ended a search for new options.

A board who is tempted to conclude that it has no choice has reached an apt time for thinking imaginatively. They believe what is familiar to be tried and true. "We know it works." Everything else is unproved and thought to be irrelevant, not useful.

Thinking imaginatively does not assume that either part of that supposition is true. Such thinking acknowledges, at least for purposes of an abstract exercise, that what is known is not sufficient. It is not sacrosanct. There is room for improvement. There are other options.

Imaginative thinking is willing to allow that some wild ideas might be useful, if not as they first appear, then in adapted form. They might be a critically useful piece for the future.

When boards don't like the alternatives which present themselves, when they are tempted to conclude that they have no choice, they ought to look beyond. They ought to look in the recycle bin. Those are the places where innovation happens. That is where you might come up with a hybrid idea.

Healthy organizations foster an environment where it is safe to try the untried, to think the unthinkable, to explore what is not fully known. Most organizations think in too confining ways. They are satisfied with what is static. They settle in. They want only what is of "our own making." Eventually, they no longer respond well to a rapidly changing environment. A board who limits its options to what it knows is likely heading for danger.

Imaginative thinking and exploring can be especially challenging for directors with long tenure. The reflex to do as has been done becomes overwhelming.

Are you under pressure to undertake an option which does not make sense to you? Is your board tempted to excuse itself by saying it really has no choice, that competition is pushing you into it? Entertain options you have discarded or refused to consider.

Are you ready to conclude you have no alternative? Consider one of Benjamin Franklin's many wise quotes; "There is a better way; find it."

Dealing with a Crisis

You are asked to attend an emergency board meeting. No details are given, but you sense that this is serious. The board assembles and the problem is explained. Looking out the window, you see the TV van parking in the drive. Tension is in the air. Blood pressures are up. Your throat is dry and your palms are wet. How should a board react? What should it do? What should it not do?

Boards are seldom required to deal with a first-rate crisis, but doing so is a board responsibility. I am embarrassed when I reflect on how poorly boards I have been part of have dealt with crises. Crisis management is clearly a subject that needs more board attention. Here are a few practical suggestions:

1) Own the problem. Don't wish it away or diminish it. Don't be embarrassed or irritated by it. It belongs to you. However disruptive and threatening it might appear, the crisis that threatens to consume you has revealed a weakness in your system, giving you an opportunity to correct it.

2) Don't overreact. Remember the first law of medicine: "Do no harm." Don't look for a scapegoat and don't lose faith. Keep a cool head. While addressing the problem, don't become consumed by it. Organizations, like athletes, need to play through their injuries.

3) Don't buy into the worst-case scenario. Things are usually not as good as they appear when they are up, nor as low as you fear when they are down. Organizations are usually more resilient than appears to be the case in a crisis. Be hopeful.

4) Make a plan to address the problem, but remember that most emergencies are not solved in one session. Begin by initiating a procedure to understand the problem, which involves hearing both sides and identifying all reasonable options.

Allowing a vacuum to develop leads to all manner of mischief. Don't attempt to squelch emotions, but don't permit them to overpower reason.

5) Consider seeking outside help. Remember, doctors who treat themselves have fools for patients. Sometimes boards are so involved in the problem, they are unable to find their way out. To know when help is needed, and then to seek it, is a sign of maturity. It is sad when good organizations lose valuable time and advantage because they are too proud or stingy to seek help.

6) Protect confidentiality, while keeping channels of communication open. Someone should be appointed to handle all official communications, and everyone else should resist the temptation to leak. Hiding will lead to speculation and suspicion. At all stages of a crisis, your various publics have a right to some information. The media can be your friend, but they must be handled wisely and discreetly.

7) Before going back to business as usually, ask yourselves how similar problems could be prevented? What have you learned from this experience, and how would you wish to respond next time? Ask yourself if some contingency planning would be useful? Open a "Crisis Management" file and keep these notes, and other helpful thoughts, to use when and if needed.

Crisis is an opportunity to become strong in your weak place.

Organizational Memory

The ability to recall is basic to human survival and advancement. If every seven years all memory were lost, civilization would still be in the Stone Age. Somebody learned something. Somebody else built on that, until we have mastered a machine that can beat us in chess. It all comes down to memory.

Computers have an amazing ability to store memory, and then to recall it instantly. Human memory is even more remarkable, although not as reliable. I know an elderly woman who knows the names, birthdays, and personality particulars of each of her 26 grandchildren and great-grandchildren. Another woman has committed her entire cookbook to memory. Humans have memory—and memories. What a gift!

Organizations need memory as much as people, and as computers, do. A lack of memory causes boards to reinvent the wheel with regularity. Ironically, some of the trickiest issues get revisited on a three- to five-year cycle. In Mennonite Central Committee we referred to them as "hardy perennials." Not only does this kind of busywork represent lost time, organizations suffer erosion in the process.

During the four years I chaired the Habitat International board, we re-examined the policy not to accept government money for housing construction several times. We hadn't forgotten, but new directors came on board and new circumstances arose which caused us to address the issue again. The danger was that familiarity with the issues tempted us to compromise. It is useful to recall what our predecessors concluded and why.

Organizational memory resides in two forms. The first is in the memory of living persons. The ability to recall names and facts is invaluable. Human memory is, however, subject to error.

It can be very selective. Memories get embellished. It is better not to bet the rent check on your memory, but memory is, nevertheless, useful. Human memory is permanently lost with the death and departure of persons with long tenure.

The second form of organizational memory is the written record. It is the more permanent and reliable form. It resides in the minute book with supporting files, including the Board Policy Manual. When you see minutes, think memory. Anyone wanting to know what an organization did 50 years ago should be able to read about it in the minute book.

Minutes, to serve their function, need to include enough detail to be understood by someone who was not present. This also gives them historical value.

The Board Policy Manual is made up of all board actions which are of a policy nature. Every board should have one. Placing such actions in a separate manual makes them available for handy reference. A Board Policy Manual helps boards be more efficient and consistent. It spares boards needing to re-examine an issue each time the board has an influx of new members.

At the center of an effective board is a reliable memory system. The lack of it results in organizational amnesia.

No More Boards!

What would happen if the earth opened up and swallowed all governing boards? If they were suddenly gone? History. Operations would continue under the direction of staff, but boards would be gone. What would be the result? Who would miss them?

An enormous cheer would go up in some quarters. I can hear it now! "We don't have this deadweight to carry around any longer. The choice space reserved for board meetings—that big room with the shiny table—can be allocated for more functional use. Those long reports we used to write, those big board books—no longer needed. Hallelujah!"

Life would go on, for a time. Gradually the euphoria would diminish. The first to notice the growing vacuum would be CEOs who could no longer draw on board members' breadth of experience and support. Members and contributors would begin to ask questions suggesting a growing distance and hinting at diminished support. Some would ask, "How do we know we can trust you?"

Gradually boards would be replaced by something akin to a board (maybe with a better name), but with some significant differences. Most boards, after a near-death experience such as just imagined, would lighten up on day-to-day details and concentrate on the future. Details take care of themselves, usually better without board involvement than with it. Micromanagement would be viewed not only as a waste of time, but as an inevitable destroyer of morale. Boards would focus on mission, on putting essential policies and reporting and evaluation procedures in place. Then they would back away and let the process work.

Instead of staying fixed only on operations, our resurrected boards would be preoccupied with the future, even though it makes them uncomfortable. Their annual plans, drawn from their long-range plans, would state clearly what they plan to accomplish. In fact, they would be driven to accomplish. "Why," they would continually ask themselves, "do we exist?" Through this thought process they would do their long-range planning, even sometimes contemplating what is still out of reach. They would set a goal and direct resources at it. At first almost imperceptibly, but, over time, it would come to pass. Surprising, you may say, but it would happen.

Our boards would provide for their own succession and that of their CEOs. They would be impatient, restless, not content to "Leave good enough alone." They would not be satisfied to dismiss the need for improvement by saying with a shrug, "If it isn't broken, don't fix it." Instead they would insist on asking, "What is wearing out, winding down? Where are we vulnerable? What will one day replace what we are now doing in this fast-paced world? What opportunities are knocking on our doors?"

Boards that work as our raised-from-the-dead board would work have a role to play. Were they to disappear, they would be sorely missed. Other less future-directed boards might be surprised at how well the work would go on without them. The question all boards need to ask themselves continually is, "Are we adding value, or are we just going along for a ride?"

Board Service Rewards

Many directors think of board service as their payback time. They have enjoyed many benefits, and now they want to do something for the good of others. That is appropriate. It is also a dilemma. St. Francis summarized the attitude well: "It is in giving that we receive." It is in serving others that we find meaning and joy in life. Yet even when our intent is to give, we are once again benefactors.

There are at least three benefits directors can legitimately expect to receive from board service.

Satisfaction

The reward for a job well done, it is said, is to have done it. After having worked hard, after having struggled and risked together, directors have a right to savor the fruits of their labors. Nothing can equal the sense of satisfaction which comes with doing good. It is appropriate to enjoy it!

Most boards don't celebrate enough. Some boards never celebrate. Some, sadly, have little to celebrate. Beware when board work gets so serious that all enjoyment is squeezed out of it, when directors get dour and humorless. When you make budget, when you fill a key staff position, when you get the permit you have been seeking, put the agenda aside and celebrate!

Personal Growth

Board service affords directors an opportunity to work alongside of, and to see into the minds of, persons to whom you would otherwise not have access. I have learned much by observing how others address issues, how they approach problems, how they absorb defeat.

Board service can be a valuable education, especially for directors who make that a conscious objective. Here is a partial list of what I have learned from fellow directors:

- Don't deal in negatives.
- Look for opportunities and be prepared to exploit them.
- Work hard; successful people usually do.
- Gather your facts, analyze and debate them vigorously, make a decision, and put it into action.
- Respect others.
- Be focused.
- Give your best and expect the best.

Friendship

My life has been enormously enriched, and my circle of friends has been expanded, by the outstanding men and women I have served with on a variety of boards. Each new board service opportunity opens the door to a new circle of friends. These friendships grow deeper as directors get better acquainted with each other while doing the work of the board. Some friendships continue long after service on that board has been terminated.

Board service is a life-expanding experience which frees us from provincialism. It helps make us more inclusive and balanced. Not infrequently, it creates opportunities for networking, with untold benefits.

Nonprofit board service does not pay well monetarily (if at all), but this is more than offset by the rewards which are, to quote a church marquee, "Out of this world."

Renewal

In their natural state, organizations are perpetually winding down. Obsolescence is a fact of life. Leaders grow old. Programs get tired and outdated. Competition is ever ready to exploit weaknesses. People of goodwill have differences which tear organizations apart.

Recognizing this is not paranoia or even undue pessimism. It is everyday reality. Unless organizations fight back, they find themselves on the proverbial slippery slope, heading toward extinction.

Organizational renewal is not only needed, it is possible. It revolves around people. Organizations are the sum of the people in them and the synergy which comes from their interaction. It is not possible to talk about organizational renewal apart from the renewal of people. The question becomes therefore, how do people bring about organizational renewal?

Closed systems do not renew themselves. They just unwind. They wear out. For renewal to happen there must be openness, reaching out, receptivity to the new. There must be striving to do things better. A holy restlessness is needed. Self-satisfied people and systems do not renew themselves.

Nothing renews like vision. The vision of something which is beyond what is being done or thought possible is essential for renewal to take place.

Urgency (distinguished from panic) is important. Time is perpetually running out. You don't have forever. Others will fill any developing vacuum. Opportunities may be lost. Like navigating a high wire, it is easier to accomplish if you are moving than if you are standing still.

Renewal involves being willing to assume risk. People and systems who won't risk won't survive. Like the proverbial frog who stays in the pail as its water grows threateningly hotter, many organizations prefer the familiar to the leap which creates new opportunities.

Renewal is an attitude. The attitude in some organizations is the antithesis of renewal. Renewal is possible only in a hopeful, positive environment.

Systems that operate as a mutual admiration society do not renew themselves. They are satisfied with things as they are. They don't even notice when things wind down.

People can change, but sometimes it is necessary to find new people. This is not to suggest a wholesale "throw out the old rascals" action. But healthy, renewing systems have a steady rotation of people coming and going. I get attached to people and hate to see them leave. We say at retirement parties, "Things will never be the same." But think about it—we don't want them to be the same.

Sometimes I become disheartened by the inefficiency and foibles of our democratic system, with the limitations of charity and development. Always, it seems, something is going wrong somewhere. Some of this is plain apathy and worse, but what heartens me is that systems are continually being renewed. The impurities keep being strained out. I have seen it. I have participated in it.

"The healthy society," says Robert K. Greenleaf, "like the health body, is not the one that takes the most medicine. It is the one in which the internal health-building forces are in the best shape."

Board Service Should Be Fun

Board meetings fun? Yes, fun! Directors should be able to look back on a year of board service and say, "I liked that! Let's do it again."

This is not to suggest that every minute of every meeting will be fun. Board and committee work can be very demanding. Getting a diverse group to agree on a complex issue can be frustrating. Boards get put into some uncomfortable situations. Sometimes the hours are long and the criticism unfair. Yet board service can also be a source of genuine satisfaction, even fun.

Board service is a pleasure when members have a sense of accomplishment. This is possible only when the board has a clear and compelling goal and some way to measure progress. Organizations who are reluctant to commit themselves to a goal, or who fear failure and so choose very modest goals, deny themselves the elation which comes with achievement.

I get frustrated when a meeting is not well planned and conducted. I don't like it when the chair allows the discussion to drift without any attempt to arrive at consensus. I am annoyed when members jump all over the place like kangaroos, with no sense of focus or discipline. Such behavior puts everyone on edge.

By way of contrast, I was privileged to participate recently in a highly rewarding committee experience. Our assignment was clear and challenging: to help a Bosnian couple move to our area. The committee was self-selected and, so, well motivated. Our meetings were relatively informal, but there was order, and members exercised good discipline. We laughed a lot. When a task was identified, it was assigned to the logical member, allowing the committee to move to the next issue. Few assignments were declined. The project was a great success. In the process the committee members forged a bond which continues to this day.

Many meetings get far too serious. Humor can be an ally, a lubricant. Be grateful if your board is blessed with a resident humorist. All boards need at least one person who can relieve a tense moment with some appropriate humor, or who can help the group laugh at itself.

Sometimes committee work is frustrating because the group attempts to do in a meeting what should have been done by one or two people before the meeting. I was known in the Habitat International board for the dictum, "No raw meat. Everything must be pre-cooked." If someone brings unprepared agenda to the table, send it back to the kitchen. Time is too short to chew on raw meat.

If your board service is not fun, if you are deriving little satisfaction from it, make a concerted effort to make your meetings more productive and enjoyable. Begin with yourself. Eventually the ripples will go out, and other will join the effort. Not only will your work be more enjoyable, it is very likely to be more effective.

Consider the advice of a friend who said, "If it isn't fun, I don't do it."

Omega

"If you know these things, blessed are you if you do them."

— Jesus (John 13:17)

My hope is that these essays have affirmed you in the many good things you, and the boards on which you serve, are doing. I also hope that you have, or that you will, identify some specific areas where you resolve to improve your performance. As Max Depree, corporate executive and author, said so helpfully, "We cannot become what we need to be by remaining what we are."

Three powerful verses from Phillips Brooks, great American hymn writer, place our board service in the context of the whole of life:

The greatest danger facing all of us is
> *not that we should make an absolute failure of life,*
> *nor that we should fall into outright licentiousness,*
> *nor that we should be terribly unhappy,*
> *nor that we will find that life has no meaning*
> > *—not any of these.*

The danger is that we may
> *fail to perceive life's greatest meaning,*
> *fall short of its highest good,*
> *miss its deepest and most abiding happiness,*
> *be unable to render the most needed service,*
> *be unconscious of life ablaze with the light of God's presence, and be content to have it so*
> > *—that is the danger.*

That some day we may wake up and find that always we have been busy with the husks and trappings of life—and have missed life itself. For life without God, to one who has known the richness and joy of life with Him, is unthinkable, impossible. That is what one prays to be spared—satisfaction with a life that falls short of the best, that has in it no tingle and thrill which comes from friendship with the Father."

A seminal quote from the great missionary humanitarian, Albert Schweitzer, reminds us that we do all need each other.

"He who has received much that is good and beautiful in life must give appropriately in return. He who is spared personal suffering must realize that he is called upon to help alleviate the suffering of others. We must all share in carrying the burden of pain laid upon the world."

About the Author

Edgar Stoesz is both a practitioner and a student/teacher of organizational theory. Having served as a CEO, responsible to a board, and on numerous and varied boards, he understands both sides of the organizational equation. The book he co-authored, *Doing Good Better* (Good Books), is used by many boards as a primer.

In addition to serving the Mennonite Central Committee in a variety of senior management roles, Stoesz has chaired numerous for-profit and nonprofit boards including Habitat for Humanity International, Hospital Albert Schweitzer, Mennonite Indemnity, and Heifer Project International. He currently chairs the board of the American Leprosy Mission.

Since co-authoring *Doing Good Better* in 1995, Stoesz has addressed or conducted workshops for more than 100 boards. He has also edited the book, *Meditations for Meetings; Thoughtful Meditations for Board Meetings and for Leaders* (Good Books).

Common Sense for Board Members
ORDER FORM

If you would like to order copies of ***Common Sense for Board Members*** for boards you know or are a part of, use this form. (Discounts apply for more than one copy.)

Photocopy this page as often as you like.

The following discounts apply:

1 copy	$8.95
2-5 copies	$8.05 each (a 10% dicount)
6-10 copies	$7.60 each (a 15% discount)
11-20 copies	$7.16 each (a 20% discount)

Prices subject to change.

Quantity   *Price*   *Total*

_____ copies of **Common Sense for Board Members**   @ _____   _____

PA residents add 6% sales tax _____

Shipping & Handling
(add 10%, $3.00 minimum) _____

TOTAL _____

(Please fill in the payment and shipping information on the other side.)

METHOD OF PAYMENT

❒ Check or Money Order
   (payable to Good Books in U.S. funds)

❒ Please charge my:
   ❒ MasterCard ❒ Visa ❒ Discover

\# _____

exp. date _____

Signature _____

Name _____

Address _____

City _____

State _____

Zip _____

Phone Number _____

SHIP TO: (if different)

Name _____

Address _____

City _____

State _____

Zip _____

Mail order to
   Good Books, P.O. Box 419, Intercourse, PA 17534-0419
   Call toll-free 800/762-7171
   Fax toll-free 888/768-3433

Prices subject to change.